T5-CQD-429

Jeff Munroe

SIGNS AND WONDERS IN THE GOSPEL OF JOHN

six unsolved mysteries

CRCPUBLICATIONS
Grand Rapids, Michigan

Unless otherwise noted, Scripture
quotations in this publication are from the
HOLY BIBLE, NEW INTERNATIONAL
VERSION, © 1973, 1978, 1984,
International Bible Society. Used by
permission of Zondervan Bible Publishers.

Prime-Time Bible Studies series. Six
Unsolved Mysteries: Signs and Wonders in
the Gospel of John, © 1997, CRC
Publications, 2850 Kalamazoo Ave. SE,
Grand Rapids, MI 49560. All rights
reserved. With the exception of brief
excerpts for review purposes, no part of
this book may be reproduced in any
manner whatsoever without written
permission from the publishers.

Printed in the U.S.A. on recycled paper. ✪
1-800-333-8300

ISBN 1-56212-262-2

10 9 8 7 6 5 4 3 2 1

Handout

TALK SHOW

Imagine a talk show on the weird topic of "What really happened at the wedding in Cana?" Further imagine that your group members are part of the show. Look through John 2:1-11 and the preparation notes for your character below.

- **Max or Maxine Dirtslinger, the host.** Your job is to keep the show moving and entertaining. Start the show by introducing the guests, one at a time, giving each guest a chance to tell what he or she saw happen at the wedding in Cana. As host, you can ask them questions if you wish. After all the guests have had their say, take your mike among the audience and give them a chance to ask questions of any of the guests. When it seems everybody has had their say, wrap up the show.

- **Daniel, the bridegroom.** You'll need to explain that in your day, the groom's family hosted a weeklong wedding feast after the wedding. Tell how you felt when the party ran out of wine, when you saw a servant drawing out washing water and taking it to the banquet master, and when the banquet master declared the ceremonial washing water a superior wine. You can't explain what happened and have not pressed for an answer, because to do so may expose your family to ridicule.

- **Saul, the banquet master.** You ran the party and were confused by the unusual practice of this family, who served the best wine last. You have no idea where the wine came from—that was the servants' job, after all. Your job was just to keep everyone happy and the party going.

- **Mary, the mother of Jesus.** You went to the wedding because Daniel, the bridegroom, is a distant relative. You heard of trouble with the wine and told your Son about it. You know that Jesus is special, and you've waited for many years for him to begin revealing that to the rest of the world. You were confident that Jesus could handle any situation, and so you were not reluctant to ask him for help.

- **Nathanael, a disciple of Jesus.** You are from Cana and grew up with Daniel. Three days before the wedding you met Jesus in spectacular fashion (read John 1:43-50). Jesus promised you that you would see great things, and at the wedding feast he kept his promise. You believe Jesus is the Messiah.

- **The studio audience.** Your job is to ask questions of the guests after they've all finished telling what they saw. For instance, you could ask the banquet master what the water in the stone jars was usually used for. You could ask which guests believe something miraculous happened. Who do the guests think Jesus is? Ask your own questions too. And, of course, you may react to any of the guests' comments as studio audiences usually do.

Handout

GOD AT WORK

■ A childhood accident had left a West Michigan man blinded in one eye. Years later, at age sixty-two, he was walking in a mall when he collided with a lamppost. All at once his vision returned and he could see clearly. At first he dismissed the idea that God had something to do with his accident. But later he had second thoughts and began attributing the recovery of his sight to God.

■ On a cold wintry night in Michigan, Evan and his friend stopped to help a young driver whose car had slid into deep snow. As they were pushing the car back onto the icy road, they failed to see another car bearing down on them, unable to stop. At the last possible second, someone (Evan knows it was an angel) led Evan to turn around. That warning gave the two men time to dive into a snowbank just before the approaching car slammed into the rear of the disabled car. Evan and his friend were unhurt. Today Evan is a minister. He says one thing that led him into the ministry was the intervention of an angel on that snowy winter night. (From _In the Company of Angels_ by Andrew Bandstra, CRC Publications.)

■ At a 1992 youth convention in Estes Park, Colorado, high school kids jammed into a meeting hall to listen to a "life challenge" that would conclude the convention. Hundreds stayed afterward to commit their lives to Christ. Meanwhile, outside, those who had left spontaneously linked hands and surrounded the huge building, singing and praying for those inside.

It was then that a sound man for a contemporary Christian group saw an amazing sight. Above the building, above the circle of kids, he saw a halo of angels. He explained later that God had given him a spirit of discernment to see what others could not see. He _knew_ that he had seen a ring of angels.

Meanwhile, the circle of kids stayed unbroken until those inside started coming out, many with tears running down their faces. (Based on an article in _The Banner,_ Sept. 14, 1992.)

Talk About It

It's not always easy to say exactly how God works in our lives. Yet God always leaves space for us to discover him in the ordinary and sometimes not-so-ordinary events of our lives.

■ In your life or the life of someone you know, have unusual events or coincidences happened that could be signs of God's working?

■ What other, perhaps more ordinary, signs do you see that God is for real?

■ One word that may summarize the miracle at Cana is "transformation." Jesus transforms the ordinary washing water into wonderful wine. He also can transform our lives from ordinary into extraordinary. What actual differences can you see that faith in Jesus makes in your life?

Handout

3 FOLLOW-UP

Journal Proposal

You are invited and encouraged to keep a personal journal for the six weeks of this course.

A journal is more than a diary that records daily events. It's a way of helping you respond to your experiences. It's a place to experiment with your thoughts. Your journal is for you alone.

Keeping a journal can really help you spiritually. Your own writing and impressions can help you see how God has brought you through life's experiences, both good and bad. A journal is also a safe place to express your doubts and struggles.

Here's the journal proposal for this week:

This week be alert for signs that God is present and working in the day-to-day events of your life. Maybe you'll see Jesus in the kindness of a friend, in a wonderful surprise, in a good time with your family, in the kind of day that makes you feel good. In your journal this week, describe one or more of these times. Tell what happened and what it showed you about God or Jesus.

For Your Devotions

This week at home, read and reflect on the miracle at Cana (John 2:1-11). Each time you read the story, imagine yourself to be a different character in it.

- First reading: you're the host who has run out of wine.
- Second reading: you're Mary, asking Jesus for help.
- Third reading: you're one of the servants whom Jesus tells to fill the jars with water.
- Fourth reading: you're Jesus, working your first miracle.

Prayer

Jesus changed the water into wine. He can also change our lives. When you look at your own life, are there areas that you wish were different? Maybe it's your relationship with your mom or dad, maybe it's a boring spiritual life, maybe you're struggling at school, or maybe it's the way you feel about yourself.

Remember God's promise in Psalm 50:3: "Our God comes and will not be silent." In your prayers this week, focus on one area for improvement. Ask God to help you make a change for the better.

Conversation

This week make an effort to talk with a parent or other relative about times when they've really seen God at work in their lives. Was it during a time of trouble or of joy? Did they realize what God was saying to them right away or much later? What did they learn about God from this experience?

Handout

4 TWO KINDS OF BREAD

After reading John 6:1-15, 25-37, quickly work through the following questions on your own. You may give more than one response to a question.

1. If you witnessed the feeding of the five thousand, how would you feel?

   a. "Incredible! What a fantastic miracle!"
   b. "Come on—there's got to be some explanation. Nobody can do what I think I just saw Jesus do."
   c. "Wow! I wonder what Jesus is going to do next? Maybe something even greater? Can't wait!"
   d. "Who is this guy, anyway?"
   e. "This is weird, spooky, mysterious!"
   f. Other?_____

2. Why did the people think Jesus was a prophet like Moses (see Deuteronomy 18:15)?

   a. Both look and act like prophets—long beard, walking stick, talk about spiritual stuff.
   b. Both were born in lowly circumstances.
   c. Both are leaders who led their people out of oppression into freedom and independence.
   d. Both miraculously fed people—Moses with manna in the wilderness, Jesus with bread and fish.
   e. Moses said another prophet who would come would be like him—that had to be Jesus.
   f. Other?_____

3. The people wanted to force Jesus to be their king. What's your reaction to this?

   a. It was stupid—why would they want to make him king?
   b. It was smart—they knew Jesus could defeat the Romans once and for all.
   c. It was understandable—we would probably have felt the same way if had we been there.
   d. Other?_____

4. How do you think Jesus felt about the people wanting to make him king?

    a. Good
    b. Angry
    c. Annoyed
    d. Sad
    e. Afraid
    f. Other?_____

5. Why did the people hunt up Jesus on the other side of the lake? What were they really interested in?

    a. They wanted more food.
    b. They wanted to see more miracles.
    c. They wanted to know why Jesus had left them sitting in the dark on the other side of the lake.
    d. They wanted Jesus to be their spiritual King.
    e. Other?_____

6. Which words describe the "bread" the people were interested in getting from Jesus?

    a. Earthly
    b. Temporary
    c. Spiritual
    d. Eternal
    e. Other?_____

7. Which words describe the "bread" Jesus offers?

    a. Earthly
    b. Temporary
    c. Spiritual
    d. Eternal
    e. Other?_____

8. What did Jesus mean when he said, "I am the bread of life"?

    a. Just as bread is good for us, believing in Jesus is good for us.
    b. Just as bread is temporary, Jesus' offer of salvation won't always be available either.
    c. Just as bread gives life to the body, Jesus gives life to our bodies and souls.
    d. Just as bread must be eaten to give life, we must make Jesus part of our lives or we will die.
    e. Other?_____

9. Jesus said that all the people had to do for "food that endures to eternal life" was to "believe in the one [God] has sent." So why didn't the people believe?

    a. Jesus was speaking in riddles again—who could know what he meant?
    b. Jesus didn't provide another "sign" for the people.
    c. Jesus called himself the bread from God, which was outrageous.
    d. Jesus didn't want to become their king.
    e. Other?_____

10. If you had been in the crowd that day, what do you really think your reaction would have been?

    a. Belief in Jesus as "the bread of life."
    b. Disbelief—more interested in things that matter here and now than in something fuzzy like "the bread of life."
    c. I really don't have a clue.
    d. Other?_____

Handout

FOLLOW-UP

Journal Proposal

Each person in the crowd who saw and tasted the miracle of the bread and fish had to answer this question: "What do you want from Jesus?" Some wanted only more of that great food that Jesus provided for free. Others probably wanted Jesus to fix whatever was wrong in their lives. Still others wanted more signs and wonders. Jesus said they could have "food that endures to eternal life" from Jesus himself if only they believed in him.

In your journal this week, reflect on what you really want from Jesus. Why are you following him? Please be honest in expressing not-so-good reasons along with the good ones.

Take some time this week to talk with Jesus about what you've written.

For Your Devotions

Read John 6 several times this week.

■ First reading: notice all the questions that people ask of Jesus.
■ Second reading: notice how Jesus answers these questions.
■ Third reading: imagine yourself in the crowd. Think of some questions you would want to ask Jesus. How do you think Jesus would answer your questions?

A New Way of Looking at Miracles

We usually think of miracles as something totally out of the realm of the ordinary. C. S. Lewis, in *The Business of Heaven,* says maybe we ought to look at *some* miracles as ordinary things done by God but greatly speeded up—kind of a shortcut to what we normally see God doing every day at slower speeds.

For example, says Lewis, think of the miracle of water changing into wine. God makes water into wine every year by "creating a vegetable organism that can turn water, soil, and sunlight into a juice which will, under proper conditions, become wine. Thus . . . he constantly turns water into wine, for wine, like all drinks, is but water modified."

At Cana, Lewis says, Christ "short-circuits the process, makes wine in a moment; uses earthenware jars instead of vegetable fibers to hold the water. But he uses them to do what he is always doing. The miracle consists in the shortcut."

Now think about the miracle of the feeding of the five thousand. Can you guess how Lewis would explain the multiplying of bread as a shortcut to what God normally does every day?

So what's the point? It's simple: Are you seeing God in the way he provides for you every day, through the normal processes of his creation? It's the same God who changed the water into wine at Cana and who fed the five thousand with a few loaves and fishes.

6 WHO'S REALLY BLIND?
(BASED ON JOHN 9)

Characters:

- Narrator
- Disciple
- Jesus
- Bart, a man born blind
- Neighbor 1
- Neighbor 2
- Pharisee 1
- Pharisee 2
- Pharisee 3
- Bart's father
- Bart's mother

Narrator: As Jesus walked along, he saw a man born blind.

Disciple: Rabbi, whose fault is it that this man was born blind? Is it because of his sin or his parents' sin?

Jesus: Neither. He is blind so that the work of God can be displayed in his life. As long as there is light, we must do the work of him who sent me. Night is coming, and no one will be able to work. While I am in the world, I am the light of the world.

Narrator: Jesus then spit on the ground, made some mud with the saliva, and put it on the man's eyes.

Jesus: Go, and wash in the pool of Siloam.

Narrator: The word *Siloam* means sent. The man followed Jesus' instructions. After washing his eyes he could see, and he went home seeing, which caused quite a stir in his neighborhood.

Neighbor 1: Hey, look, it's Bart, the blind man who used to sit and beg. Look at him—he can see.

Neighbor 2: That isn't Bart—that's only someone who looks like him.

Bart: No, it's really me.

Neighbor 1: How can you see? What happened?

Bart: The man they call Jesus made mud and put it on my eyes. Then he told me to go to Siloam and wash. So I did it, and now I can see.

Neighbor 2: Where is this man Jesus?

Bart: I don't know.

Neighbor 1: This is unheard of. We had better take you to the Pharisees.

Narrator: So they took Bart to the Pharisees. Now the day that Jesus had made the mud and healed Bart was a Sabbath. Jewish law prohibited mixing dirt with water to make mud on the Sabbath, and it prohibited healing non-life-threatening problems on the Sabbath. So the Pharisees were both curious and disturbed.

Pharisee 1 (to Bart): How did you receive your sight?

Bart: Jesus put mud on my eyes, I washed, and now I see.

Pharisee 2: This is a clear violation of the Sabbath. Jesus cannot be from God.

Pharisee 3: But how can a sinner do such marvelous signs?

Narrator: So there was a split in the ranks of the Pharisees. They argued back and forth. Finally, they decided to go interrogate the blind man himself.

Pharisee 1 (to Bart): So what do *you* say about Jesus? You're the one he healed.

Bart: He's a prophet.

Pharisee 2: How do we know any of this is true? Maybe we're being set up here. Does anyone know this man? Has anyone thought that he's just spinning a story to embarrass us? How do we know he was really born blind?

Pharisee 3: We could ask his parents.

Narrator: So they sent for his parents, who were afraid of the Pharisees, for they had heard that anyone who believed that Jesus was the Messiah would be kicked out of the synagogue for life.

Pharisee 1 (to Bart's parents): Is this your son?

Bart's father: Yes.

Pharisee 2: Was he really born blind?

Bart's mother: Yes.

Pharisee 3: Well, then how can he see?

Bart's father: We know he is our son.

Bart's mother: And we know he was born blind.

Bart's father: But we don't know how it is that he can now see.

Bart's mother: And we especially don't know who did it.

Bart's father: Why are you asking us? We didn't do this to him. We don't want any trouble. Why don't you ask him? He's an adult; he can speak for himself.

Narrator: So the Pharisees decided to interrogate Bart a second time.

Pharisee 1: In the name of God tell the truth this time. You know as well as we do that this Jesus is a sinner.

Bart: I don't know if he's a sinner or not. I am not an educated person like all of you are, and besides, I couldn't see anything. This is what I do know for sure—I used to be blind and now I can see.

Pharisee 2: He sinned when he healed you. What did he do to you? How did he heal you?

Bart: I told you already how he healed me. Didn't you listen? Why do you keep asking me about this? Do you want to become his disciples too?

Pharisee 3: *You're* his disciple, not us! We are disciples of Moses! We *know* that God spoke to Moses—but as for your Jesus, well, there are a lot of rumors about him. Let's just say that we are not too sure about his origins.

Bart: Well, that is remarkable. You don't know about him, and yet he can open my eyes. You see a miracle in front of you, and you refuse to accept that it has happened. You pretend to know so much about God and who is a sinner and who isn't. Let me tell you, if Jesus were a sinner, he couldn't have healed me—for even I know that God doesn't listen to sinners. Nobody has ever heard of opening the eyes of a blind person. No one—ever! If this man were not from God, this could not have happened!

Pharisee 1: Who do you think you are, anyway?

Pharisee 2: You're trash, that's what! You were full of sin the day you were born.

Pharisee 3: How do you—a sinner—dare lecture us?

Narrator: So the Pharisees threw him out. But when Jesus heard about this, he went and found him.

Jesus: Do you believe in the Son of Man?

Bart: Tell me who he is so that I might believe in him.

Jesus: You've heard him speak before, and now you are seeing him face to face.

Bart: Lord, I believe.

Jesus: For judgment I have come into this world, so the blind will see and those who see will become blind.

Narrator: Some Pharisees who were with Jesus heard him say this.

Pharisee 1: What are you saying? Surely you are not saying that we are blind.

Jesus: If you were blind, you would be like Bart and not guilty of sinning. But since you claim that you can see, your own words convict you and your guilt remains.

Talk About It

1. Jesus knew that the Pharisees would consider his healing this blind man as breaking the Sabbath. Why do you think he did things that he knew would bother them?

2. Why are some of the man's neighbors and the Pharisees so unwilling to accept this miracle?

3. Use your Bible to trace how the healed man grows in his understanding of who Jesus is.

4. How do the events in this story illustrate what Jesus says at the end, that "for judgment I have come into this world, so that the blind will see and those who see will become blind"?

5. In what ways are we sometimes like the blind man who was healed?

6. In what ways are we sometimes like the Pharisees?

7 HELPING EACH OTHER SEE

	known to self	not known to self
known others	I Open	II Blind
not known to others	III Hidden	IV Unknown

Above is a picture of a group-dynamics theory called Johari's window, which is divided into four quadrants or parts. Joe and Harry, the creators of Johari's window, depicted four areas of our lives:

I. There are parts of our lives that are known both to us and to others—our public behaviors that all observe.

II. There are parts of our lives that others see but that we are blind to. This is sometimes called the "bad breath" area. Others always know we have bad breath before we do.

III. There are parts of our lives that we know but that we hide from others. We hide these things because we think that if others knew these things about us they would not like us.

IV. There are parts of our lives that we do not know and that others do not know. This is often called the "unconscious" area.

Joe and Harry said that whenever people form a group, the size of the first window is small, but as the group progresses and trust builds, three things can happen. First, I may share something personal about myself, which makes quadrant I larger and quadrant III smaller. Then others may share an observation about me, which makes quadrant I larger and quadrant II smaller. Finally, together we may make some "aha!" discoveries that reduce the size of quadrant IV.

Talk About It

Is there truth here about God?

■ Is it possible that in some ways the work of God acting in and through our lives falls into quadrant II, so that it is sometimes easier seen by others that it is by ourselves?

■ How do you see God in the other members of your group?

In a few moments, you will have a chance to hear how others see God acting in you and to tell others in your group how you see God acting in them. This is a chance for you to help others see how God works in and through their lives.

FOLLOW-UP

Journal Proposal

In today's story, the Pharisees thought they had perfect vision, but they turned out to be spiritually blind. And the blind man turned out to have the best vision of all!

Think about your own "spiritual vision." Would you say it's 20/20? Or are there some blind spots? Some blurriness here and there? Some places where you wish you could see more clearly?

Jot down your reflections on these questions in your journal. In your prayers this week, ask for clearer vision to "see Jesus" in those troublesome areas of your life.

For Your Devotions

John 9 is one of the best-told stories in the gospels. Read it through several times this week:

- First reading: imagine yourself as the blind man.
- Second reading: imagine yourself as the Pharisees.
- Third reading: jot down any questions you would like to ask Jesus about this miracle.

Something to Think About

People in Jesus' day found it no easier to believe in miracles than do people in our modern, skeptical age. The Pharisees in John 9 held a formal inquiry in order to disprove the blind man's story. Most astonishingly, the Roman soldiers who witnessed the greatest miracle, the resurrection, experienced no great change of heart—instead, they changed their story in return for a payoff. . . .

Jesus never met a disease he could not cure, a birth defect he could not reverse, a demon he could not exorcise. But he did meet skeptics he could not convince and sinners he could not convert.

—Philip Yancey, "Jesus, the Reluctant Miracle Worker,"
Christianity Today, May 19, 1997.

IS IT DEAD?

The following excerpt is from *My Name Is Asher Lev* by Chaim Potok (Alfred A.Knopf, Inc., 1972. Used by permission).

(In the story, Asher and his father have just seen a bird next to the curb on their way home from Sabbath services.)

"Is it dead, Papa?" I was six and could not bring myself to look at it.

"Yes," I heard him say in a sad and distant way.

"Why did it die?"

"Everything that lives must die."

"Everything?"

"Yes."

"You too, Papa? And Mama?"

"Yes."

"And me?"

"Yes," he said. Then he added in Yiddish, "But may it be only after you live a long and good life, my Asher."

I could not grasp it. I forced myself to look at the bird. Everything alive would be one day as still as that bird?

"Why?" I asked.

"That's the way Ribbono Shelolom made His world, Asher."

"Why?"

"So life would be precious, Asher. Something that is yours forever is never precious."

Handout

10 RESURRECTION REALITIES

The resurrection of Jesus Christ changes the way we understand things. Below is a list of some of the things that his resurrection changes. In the left column, fill in how we would think about each item if the resurrection had never happened. In the right column, fill in how we think about each item because the resurrection has happened. The first one has been partially completed for you.

	Resurrection								
No Resurrection	*The end of life*								
	Death	**Life**	**Suffering**	**Christ**	**Salvation**	**Stress**	**Money**	**Grades**	**Future Job**

Handout

11 FOLLOW-UP

Journal Proposal

There's no greater miracle than the raising of someone from the dead—and that's exactly what Jesus did, first for Lazarus, then later for himself and for us. This week, think about what Christ's resurrection means to you. You may want to use these sentence starters as you write in your journal:

■ If Jesus had not risen from the dead, my life would be . . .
■ Because Jesus has risen from the dead, I . . .

For Your Devotions

John 11 can be divided into several sections. Read each section and think about the questions that follow.

■ Read John 11:1-16. Why did Jesus delay in answering Mary and Martha's request? Does this help you understand why God sometimes delays his answers to your prayers?

■ Read John 11:17-37. Mary and Martha both ask Jesus the same question: "Where were you when we needed you?" Has this ever been your question of God? If so, how did God answer?

■ Read John 11:38-44. Imagine yourself witnessing this great miracle. What would you say or do?

■ Read John 11:45-57. How did people respond to Jesus' raising of Lazarus? What does this miracle show you about Jesus?

"Just Like Job" by Maya Angelou

You may want to use this poem as your prayer this week at home. Before you read the poem, check out Job 23:3-5, 8-9.

My Lord, my Lord,
Long have I cried out to Thee
In the heat of the sun,
The cool of the moon,
My screams searched the heavens for Thee.
My God,
When my blanket was nothing but dew,
Rags and bones
Were all I owned,
I chanted Your name
Just like Job.

Father, Father,
My life give I gladly to Thee
Deep rivers ahead
High mountains above
My soul wants only Your love
But fears gather round like wolves in the dark.
Have You forgotten my name?
O Lord, come to Your child.
O Lord, forget me not.

You said to lean on Your arm
And I'm leaning
You said to trust in Your love
And I'm trusting
You said to call on Your name
And I'm calling
I'm stepping out on Your word.

You said You'd be my protection,
My only and glorious savior,
My beautiful Rose of Sharon,
And I'm stepping out on Your word.
Joy, joy
Your word.
Joy, joy
The wonderful word of the Son of God.

You said that You would take me to glory
To sit down at the welcome table
Rejoice with my mother in heaven
And I'm stepping out on Your word.

Into the alleys
Into the byways
Into the streets
And the roads
And the highways
Past rumor mongers
And midnight ramblers
Past the liars and the cheaters and the gamblers
On Your word
On Your word.
On the wonderful word of the Son of God.
I'm stepping out on Your word.

—from *And Still I Rise* by Maya Angelou, ©1978 by Maya Angelou.
Reprinted by permission of Random House, Inc.

Taken from **THE BOOK OF GOD** by Walter Wangerin, Jr. Copyright 1995 by Walter Wangerin, Jr. Used by permission of Zondervan Publishing House.

Early Sunday morning, as soon as the Sabbath restrictions were lifted and they could in good conscience travel distances, three women left Bethany for Jerusalem: Mary Magdalene, Mary Salome, and Joanna.

Midway around the northern rise of the Mount of Olives, Mary Magdalene stopped and looked at the others.

"Did you feel that?" she said. "Did the earth tremble?"

Each woman was carrying cloths and a jar in her arms, myrrh in one, frankincense, nard. They meant to anoint the corpse of the Lord with spices, their final honor to him whom they loved. It was only the third day since he had been buried.

"It seemed that the ground moved under my feet."

"It *did* move," said Joanna.

Mary Salome said, "But there was no sound."

Neither was there light yet, though the stars were dimming in a charcoal sky. Dawn was behind them.

"Let's go."

"Hurry. Please hurry."

They skirted Jerusalem on its northern side, then turned south to the garden in which Joseph's tomb had been newly hewn in rock. Mary Magdalene was peering forward and muttering, "But who will roll the stone?" She couldn't make out which sepulcher was Joseph's. The wall of the city was on their left, blocking any eastern light. All the tombs were in shadow.

Suddenly Joanna shrieked and dropped her jar.

Mary Salome dropped hers too. It shattered.

A pillar of white light, bright as a blade, had shot down from heaven and stood on the stone of Joseph's tomb. That stone was lying flat on the ground.

Mary Magdalene gasped. The dawn air smelled of myrrh.

A voice said: *Don't be afraid.*

It seemed to Mary that the light contained the figure of a man, glorious in every aspect and so bright that brightness itself was his clothing.

The man said, *You seek Jesus of Nazareth, who was crucified. He is not here. Behold the place where they laid him. Then run to tell his disciples that he goes before you into Galilee. There you shall see him as he said to you.*

The light withdrew into heaven, leaving the women blinded and terrified. That voice had been no consolation.

Mary Salome gathered her robe up and started to run back the way that they had come.

Mary Magdalene, void of all expression, began moving toward the tomb itself.

"Mary, *don't!*" Joanna rushed forward and pulled at her sleeve, but then she shrank back from the open tomb, wailing, "Mary, please! It was an earthquake! It was the Romans or the wrath of God. Whatever happened, it's all over now. Mary, please, let's go!"

Mary did not respond. The small, solemn, pale woman now knelt down directly in front of the black hole in stone.

This was more than Joanna could bear. "We can't tell *anyone,*" she cried, and dashed after Mary Salome.

Mary Magdalene bent forward and stretched her hand into the shadow of the sepulcher. Cold air. A dead air, but no odor. On the right side in darkness she touched a flank of hewn stone. With her fingers' tips she measured upward one cubit and came to its surface: this was the ledge upon which they had laid the body of the Lord. She reached deeper in darkness, preparing to touch his rigid corpse—but found nothing. Felt nothing. There was nothing there.

Mary's stomach twisted. He was *gone!* He *was* gone, as the blinding white figure had said!

Mary jumped up.

Daybreak: there were flecks of golden fire over Jerusalem, south between the stone wall and the hill of crosses. She ran through the Garden Gate into the city and up the road that led to Zion. She ran to the house of the Essene and beat on his door. She beat and beat until someone came and opened it. Then she rushed through the vestibule, out the back to a second building built higher than the first, up its stairs to another door, which was locked: "Simon!" she cried. "Simon! Simon, open the door!"

Not since Jesus had driven the demons out of her had Mary moved with such strength and ferocity. If Simon didn't open the door soon, she had a mind to crack it like a cask with her forehead. *Behold, Mary! Mary Magdalene is crazy again!*

But Simon did open the door.

And Mary immediately was chattering: "They took the Lord out of the tomb, out of the *tomb*, Simon, Joseph's tomb, the tomb itself, and we don't know where they put him—"

Simon grabbed her and demanded, "Are you sure?"

Mary said, "It was dark, but I put my hand in —"

But Simon Peter was already racing down the steps and out into the street.

John cried, "Simon, I'm coming, too." He flew past Mary. He ran so fast that he outdistanced Simon.

Mary followed both men. She caught up to Simon at the Garden Gate, and when they both came to the tomb they found John kneeling at the entrance peering into it.

Simon pushed John aside and went in.

The morning light had strengthened. Mary could see what Simon Peter was looking at inside: the shroud — still in its windings on the ledge, but flat. And there was the cloth that had covered Jesus' head, rolled up in a place by itself.

Now John, too, crawled into the tomb. The two men crowded the small space, so Mary pulled back and stood aside, shifting her weight from foot to foot.

When the men came out they were shaking their heads and saying nothing.

"Simon?" Mary begged. "John?"

But they began to walk away, each consumed by his own thoughts.

Mary ran ahead and stood directly in front of Simon Peter. "What are you going to do about it?" she said. "How will we find his body?"

Simon put his big face close to hers. She saw his jowls trembling. "Leave it alone!" he said. "Don't you think we're in enough danger already?" Then he walked away. John followed.

Mary watched until they disappeared into the city and then, finally, she began to cry.

No, Mary Magdalene was not strong again. She was weak and helpless and sad and desolate. And now that the tears had begun, she could not control herself at all. She went to the place where Mary Salome had broken her jar of myrrh. She knelt down and gathered the pieces and tried to fit them together again. But she couldn't. She could hardly *see*. Weeping filled her vision with such a rain of sorrow, that all the world was blurred.

She dropped the clay shards and howled like a small child lost. *Yes, Mary is crazy again, and she doesn't care. She doesn't care.*

"Woman?"

Someone was calling to her.

"Woman?" It was a clear voice, breaking through the morning and the roaring in her head.

"Woman," it said, "why are you weeping?"

Huffing with her sobs, Mary looked up and thought she saw the gardener coming.

"Because they took my Lord away," she sobbed, "and I don't know where they put him."

The man said, "Who are you looking for?"

"Oh, sir!" Mary said, rising up. "If you are the one who carried him off, tell me where he is and I'll get him myself."

Now the man stopped directly in front of her—long, dark hair through her swim of tears. A white tunic. Clean-shaven.

In a soft, familiar voice, the man said, "Oh, Mary."

She gasped.

She looked and saw the beautiful forehead, the raven black hair of her dear Lord Jesus and his steadfast, golden gaze!

"*Rabboni!*" she cried.

"Hush, hush, child — hush." Jesus placed a finger to his lips. "You cannot cling to me now," he said. "I haven't yet ascended to my Father. But go to my friends and tell them that I am ascending to my Father and your Father, to my God and your God."

Oh, yes, Mary Magdalene was very strong indeed, and swifter than the north wind blowing toward Jerusalem. She was fair and she was lovely now, her lips like a scarlet thread, her cheeks like halves of a pomegranate.

The morning was still young when she arrived for the second time at the upper room and stood in the doorway laughing into the dark den of gloomy disciples.

Mary couldn't help herself. It was his great grim mouth that drove her to it. She threw out her arms and ran to Simon Peter crying: "Simon, dance with me! Hug me and spin me around, because I have just seen the Lord. *He is alive!* Simon, Simon, he has risen from the dead!"

Handout

13 FOLLOW-UP

Journal Proposal

Every Christian, how matter how strong his or her faith, has moments of doubt; in fact, God uses our doubts to teach us to trust more completely in him, to strengthen our faith. This week use your journal to reflect on your own feelings of doubt. What questions, if any, do you have about your faith? About God? About Jesus? About Christianity in general?

Thomas had his doubts but made one of the greatest confessions in all of Scripture when he said to Jesus, "My Lord and my God!" (John 20:28). Now that you've reflected on your doubts, think about what you know and believe about Jesus. Jot down some of these statements of faith that the Holy Spirit has convinced you are true.

For Your Devotions

This week read John 20 several times. Think of questions that you would like to ask Mary, Peter, Thomas, and Jesus. Think about one question that you would like to ask God about your faith-life. Then ask him that question in your prayers this week.

John 20:31 is the key verse in the gospel of John. It tells why John wrote his gospel and gives us the ultimate reason for reading the Bible. It's a verse you may want to memorize and keep for life.

Conversation

Talk with an adult whom you regard as a strong Christian. Ask that person what helps him or her get through times of trouble and doubt. Jot down his or her advice and refer to it when the doubts get to you.

Want to Trade Places?

Frederick Buechner writes, "Even though [Jesus] said the greater blessing is for those who can believe without seeing [John 20:29], it's hard to imagine that there's a believer anywhere who wouldn't have traded places with Thomas, given the chance, and seen that face and heard that voice and touched those ruined hands."

Think about that. Do you agree? Why or why not?

14 ANY ALLIGATORS IN YOUR LAKE?

An old woman once lived on the shore of a lake in southern Florida. Other residents in the area warned the woman that a large alligator lived in the lake. But the woman decided not to worry about it. She figured that if she left it alone, it wouldn't bother her. So for many years she ignored the alligator. She did not watch for the gator and acted as if it didn't exist.

One day the old woman was washing some things in the lake. Suddenly, without warning of any kind, the gator appeared from nowhere and struck hard at the woman's arm. In an instant her hand was snapped off. She was fortunate to escape with her life.

Terrified, she ran into the house and called an ambulance. Later that afternoon, wildlife officials arrived, found a gator, and killed it. To be sure they had killed the right gator, they cut its stomach open. Inside was the old woman's hand.

A wildlife official told the press after the incident that the assumption the old woman made—that ignoring the alligator would protect her from attack—was the opposite of the truth. Ignoring the gator, the official said, only made it more likely that one day it would attack her. With the passing of time, the gator became less and less frightened of the woman. With fear taken out of the picture, it only became a matter of opportunity before the alligator struck.

Handout

75 A LAKESIDE ENCOUNTER

The Story

Use your Bible (John 21) as you work through these questions. You may give more than one response to a question if you wish.

1. What does the fact that the disciples go fishing tell you?

   a. They want to have some fun.
   b. They are broke and need to catch and sell some fish.
   c. They have decided to go back to their pre-Jesus life.
   d. They love fishing more than they love Jesus.
   e. Other?_____

2. After fishing all night, the disciples catch nothing. Then, on advice from a stranger, they catch so many they can't haul in their net. If I had been fishing with them, I would have thought—

   a. "I wonder who that guy is who gave us such good advice?"
   b. "I guess our luck took a turn for the better."
   c. "This is unbelievable! Fantastic! How can it be?"
   d. "Only Jesus could work a miracle like this."
   e. "Can't wait to sell all these fish!"
   f. Other?_____

3. When John says, "It is the Lord," Peter jumps in and starts swimming for shore. Why?

   a. He knows the boat will sink when all those fish are hauled in.
   b. He can't wait to see Jesus—they have lots to talk about.
   c. He wants to show Jesus he's still the leader of the disciples.
   d. He's just happy to see Jesus.
   e. Other?_____

4. The disciples do not dare ask the man on the beach who he is. Why not?

   a. They're not sure it's the Lord.
   b. They're in awe of him.
   c. They don't want to embarrass themselves.
   d. They're afraid of being reprimanded for asking.
   e. Other?_____

5. John reports Jesus' miracles as signs that have several meanings. Of what might the great catch of fish be a sign? (John 5:15 may provide a clue.)

    a. Without Jesus, we can't do anything; with him, all things are possible.
    b. Jesus changes our luck from bad to good.
    c. Always listen to Jesus.
    d. It's time for the disciples to get on with their mission: becoming fishers of men.
    e. Other?_____

6. Why does Jesus ask Peter "Do you love me?" not once but three times?

    a. To make sure Peter (and the other disciples) get the connection to the three times Peter denied Jesus.
    b. To make Peter squirm a little.
    c. To show Peter (and the other disciples) that Peter was completely forgiven and restored.
    d. To emphasize that the most important question anyone can be asked is "Do you love Jesus?"
    e. Other?_____

7. I imagine Peter answering Jesus—

    a. Loudly, confidently, boldly
    b. Softly, humbly, urgently
    c. Reluctantly, as if angry or upset
    d. Other?_____

8. What shows that Jesus hasn't given up on Peter?

    a. He asks Peter, "Do you love me?"
    b. He gives Peter something important to do ("feed my sheep").
    c. He restores Peter in front of the other disciples.
    d. He tells Peter to follow him.
    e. Other?_____

9. "Feed my sheep" means—

    a. Become a shepherd—it pays better than fishing.
    b. Give people food when they're hungry.
    c. Tell people the good news about Jesus.
    d. Help people grow in their relationship to God.
    e. Other?_____

10. After this encounter, Peter probably felt—

    a. Worried that he might be crucified like Jesus.
    b. Relieved that Jesus wasn't angry with him.
    c. Humbly grateful for being forgiven, restored.
    d. Proud of the important work he had been given to do.
    e. Ready to do his job as leader of the disciples.
    f. Other?_____

My Story

■ If Jesus looked at your life this week, would he need to ask: "Do you love me?"

■ As the gospel of John closes, Jesus gives clear directions to Peter ("feed my sheep" and "follow me"). What direction might Jesus be giving you as our study of John ends?

FOLLOW-UP

Journal Proposal

You can't sink any lower than Peter did—first bragging that he'd follow Jesus to the death, then swearing up and down that he had never heard of the man. After his denial, macho Peter "broke down and wept" (Mark 14:72). He needed a second chance—and Jesus gave it to him, gently forgiving him, restoring him, healing his hurts.

Even the best of Christians need second chances—lots and lots of them! This week reflect on an area of your life in which you feel the need for the forgiving and healing touch of Jesus. Jot down your thoughts in your journal and take them to God in prayer.

Remember what John wrote in one of his letters: "If we confess our sin, he is faithful and just and will forgive us our sins" (1 John 1:9).

For Your Devotions

We can learn a lot from reading about the life of Peter, a very human disciple who also learned a great deal from the time when Jesus first said "follow me" to the time of his own death as a Christian martyr. Trace Peter's career as described by John:

- John 1:35-42   Calling and naming
- John 6:60-71   A decision to stick
- John 13:1-17   Peter says no to Jesus
- John 13:31-38   A little bragging
- John 18:15-18, 25-27 A very big failure
- John 20:3-9   A race to a tomb
- John 21:15-19   A second chance

Praying ACTS

Ever feel like your prayers sort of ramble from one topic to another, finally ending with an "Amen" when you can't think of anything else to say? Ever feel that most of your prayers consist of asking God for things?

Many Christians use the ACTS method to organize and balance their prayers. ACTS stands for adoration, confession, thanksgiving, and supplication.

■ **Adoration:** Begin your prayer by honoring or worshiping God for who he is. Unlike *thanksgiving,* which focuses on what he has done, *adoration* focuses on God's attributes (for example, God is holy, wise, just, loving, and unchanging). So begin your prayer by telling God why you worship him. It may help to look at the Psalms for ideas—for example, see Psalm 89:1-18, Psalm 97, and Psalm 99. You could begin your prayer time with one of these psalms. Just read it to God as your prayer. Then add personal words of adoration.

■ **Confession:** James 5:16 and 1 John 1:8-10 speak of the power of confessing our sins to both God and each other. Healing happens after confession. Take time to confess your sins to God, not just generally ("forgive all my many, many sins") but specifically ("please forgive me for hurting my best friend today").

■ **Thanksgiving:** God has done great things! God loves to hear us say "thank you." Be sure to thank God for his forgiveness.

■ **Supplication:** This means humbly asking God for something. Too often we just take our requests to God as if he is Santa Claus. An ACTS prayer helps us put our requests in their proper place—after we have worshiped, confessed, and thanked God, then we can approach him with our requests. As you consider his call to "feed my sheep" and "follow me," where do you need his help?

EVALUATION FORM

Please check the items that describe your group sessions:

☐ interesting
☐ boring
☐ too easy
☐ too hard
☐ about the right difficulty
☐ related to my daily life
☐ unrelated to my daily life
☐ dominated by leader
☐ good group participation, discussion
☐ other:_____

Please check those activities you like best:

☐ working in small groups
☐ discussing with the whole group
☐ dramatizing the Bible stories
☐ using the handouts
☐ praying together
☐ reading/studying the Bible on my own
☐ writing by myself or with others
☐ drawing and other artistic responses
☐ other:_____

During the week at home I—

☐ did not do any of the follow-up activities (journal, daily devotions, readings)
☐ did some of these activities
☐ did most of the activities

Please check the items that tell what you gained from this course:

☐ better understanding of and appreciation for the miracles in the gospel of John
☐ deeper understanding of what the miracles tell us about Jesus
☐ some growth in my relationship with others and with God
☐ other:_____

In general, I would rate this course as

☐ excellent
☐ good
☐ fair
☐ poor

If you could change anything about this course, what would it be? Please comment and add anything else that's on your mind.

Name (optional): _____

Age or school grade: _____

Male or female: _____

Church: _____

City/State/Province: _____

Please send completed forms to

CRC Publications
Prime-Time Bible Studies
2850 Kalamazoo Ave. SE
Grand Rapids, MI 49560

Thank you!